50 Healthy Salads Ready in 15 Minutes

By: Kelly Johnson

Table of Contents

- Greek Salad
- Caprese Salad
- Quinoa Salad with Black Beans and Corn
- Chickpea Salad with Cucumber and Feta
- Spinach and Strawberry Salad
- Avocado and Tomato Salad
- Tuna Salad with Mixed Greens
- Apple and Walnut Salad
- Cabbage and Carrot Slaw
- Mediterranean Couscous Salad
- Lentil Salad with Bell Peppers
- Arugula Salad with Pears and Goat Cheese
- Thai Cucumber Salad
- Bulgur Wheat Salad with Cherry Tomatoes
- Broccoli and Raisin Salad
- Roasted Beet and Feta Salad
- Zucchini Noodle Salad with Pesto
- Kale Salad with Lemon and Olive Oil
- Cucumber and Avocado Salad
- Pasta Salad with Spinach and Sun-Dried Tomatoes
- Chopped Salad with Italian Dressing
- Citrus Salad with Grapefruit and Orange
- Asian Noodle Salad
- Berry Spinach Salad with Almonds
- Sweet Potato and Black Bean Salad
- Cabbage and Apple Salad
- Roasted Chickpea Salad
- Corn and Tomato Salad
- Hummus and Veggie Salad
- Pea Salad with Bacon and Cheese
- Carrot and Raisin Salad
- Fruit Salad with Mint
- Fattoush Salad
- Radish and Cucumber Salad
- Smashed Chickpea Salad

- Mediterranean Orzo Salad
- Tomato and Mozzarella Salad
- Spicy Kale Salad with Tahini Dressing
- Egg Salad with Spinach
- Sesame Ginger Salad
- Roasted Vegetable Salad
- Nicoise Salad
- Taco Salad with Ground Turkey
- Rice Salad with Peas and Carrots
- Quinoa Tabbouleh
- Lime Chicken Salad
- Chopped Greek Salad
- Pineapple and Avocado Salad
- Zesty Lime Shrimp Salad
- Mango and Black Bean Salad

Greek Salad

Ingredients:

- 2 cups chopped cucumbers
- 2 cups chopped tomatoes
- 1 cup Kalamata olives
- 1 cup feta cheese, crumbled
- 1/2 red onion, thinly sliced
- 1/4 cup olive oil
- 2 tbsp red wine vinegar
- 1 tsp dried oregano
- Salt and pepper to taste

Instructions:

1. In a large bowl, combine cucumbers, tomatoes, olives, feta cheese, and red onion.
2. In a small bowl, whisk together olive oil, red wine vinegar, oregano, salt, and pepper.
3. Drizzle dressing over the salad and toss gently to combine.

Caprese Salad

Ingredients:

- 4 ripe tomatoes, sliced
- 8 oz fresh mozzarella cheese, sliced
- Fresh basil leaves
- 1/4 cup olive oil
- Balsamic vinegar (for drizzling)
- Salt and pepper to taste

Instructions:

1. On a serving platter, alternate layers of tomato slices, mozzarella slices, and basil leaves.
2. Drizzle olive oil and balsamic vinegar over the top.
3. Season with salt and pepper before serving.

Quinoa Salad with Black Beans and Corn

Ingredients:

- 1 cup cooked quinoa
- 1 cup black beans, rinsed and drained
- 1 cup corn (fresh, frozen, or canned)
- 1 red bell pepper, diced
- 1/4 cup chopped cilantro
- 1 lime, juiced
- 1/4 cup olive oil
- Salt and pepper to taste

Instructions:

1. In a large bowl, combine cooked quinoa, black beans, corn, red bell pepper, and cilantro.
2. In a small bowl, whisk together lime juice, olive oil, salt, and pepper.
3. Pour the dressing over the salad and toss gently to combine.

Chickpea Salad with Cucumber and Feta

Ingredients:

- 1 can chickpeas, rinsed and drained
- 1 cup diced cucumber
- 1/2 cup cherry tomatoes, halved
- 1/4 cup feta cheese, crumbled
- 1/4 red onion, finely chopped
- 2 tbsp olive oil
- 1 tbsp lemon juice
- Salt and pepper to taste

Instructions:

1. In a large bowl, combine chickpeas, cucumber, cherry tomatoes, feta cheese, and red onion.
2. In a small bowl, whisk together olive oil, lemon juice, salt, and pepper.
3. Drizzle the dressing over the salad and toss gently to combine.

Spinach and Strawberry Salad

Ingredients:

- 4 cups fresh spinach
- 1 cup sliced strawberries
- 1/4 cup sliced almonds
- 1/4 cup feta cheese, crumbled
- 2 tbsp balsamic vinaigrette

Instructions:

1. In a large bowl, combine spinach, strawberries, almonds, and feta cheese.
2. Drizzle with balsamic vinaigrette and toss gently to combine.

Avocado and Tomato Salad

Ingredients:

- 2 ripe avocados, diced
- 2 cups cherry tomatoes, halved
- 1/4 red onion, thinly sliced
- 1 lime, juiced
- 1/4 cup olive oil
- Salt and pepper to taste

Instructions:

1. In a large bowl, combine avocados, cherry tomatoes, and red onion.
2. Drizzle with lime juice and olive oil.
3. Season with salt and pepper and toss gently to combine.

Tuna Salad with Mixed Greens

Ingredients:

- 1 can tuna, drained
- 4 cups mixed greens
- 1/4 cup diced celery
- 1/4 cup mayonnaise
- 1 tbsp Dijon mustard
- Salt and pepper to taste

Instructions:

1. In a bowl, combine tuna, celery, mayonnaise, and Dijon mustard.
2. In a large bowl, toss mixed greens with salt and pepper.
3. Serve the tuna salad over the mixed greens.

Apple and Walnut Salad

Ingredients:

- 2 cups mixed greens
- 1 apple, sliced
- 1/2 cup walnuts, toasted
- 1/4 cup feta cheese, crumbled
- 2 tbsp balsamic vinaigrette

Instructions:

1. In a large bowl, combine mixed greens, apple slices, walnuts, and feta cheese.
2. Drizzle with balsamic vinaigrette and toss gently to combine.

Cabbage and Carrot Slaw

Ingredients:

- 4 cups shredded cabbage
- 2 cups grated carrots
- 1/2 cup mayonnaise
- 2 tbsp apple cider vinegar
- 1 tbsp sugar
- Salt and pepper to taste

Instructions:

1. In a large bowl, combine shredded cabbage and grated carrots.
2. In a separate bowl, whisk together mayonnaise, apple cider vinegar, sugar, salt, and pepper.
3. Pour the dressing over the cabbage and carrots, and toss to combine.

Mediterranean Couscous Salad

Ingredients:

- 1 cup couscous
- 1 1/4 cups vegetable broth
- 1 cup cherry tomatoes, halved
- 1/2 cup cucumber, diced
- 1/4 cup red onion, diced
- 1/4 cup Kalamata olives, sliced
- 1/4 cup feta cheese, crumbled
- 2 tbsp olive oil
- 1 tbsp lemon juice
- Salt and pepper to taste

Instructions:

1. In a pot, bring vegetable broth to a boil and add couscous. Cover and remove from heat. Let it sit for 5 minutes, then fluff with a fork.
2. In a large bowl, combine couscous, cherry tomatoes, cucumber, red onion, olives, and feta cheese.
3. In a small bowl, whisk together olive oil, lemon juice, salt, and pepper. Pour over the salad and toss gently to combine.

Lentil Salad with Bell Peppers

Ingredients:

- 1 cup cooked lentils
- 1 cup diced bell peppers (red, yellow, green)
- 1/4 cup red onion, finely chopped
- 2 tbsp olive oil
- 1 tbsp red wine vinegar
- 1 tsp Dijon mustard
- Salt and pepper to taste

Instructions:

1. In a large bowl, combine cooked lentils, bell peppers, and red onion.
2. In a small bowl, whisk together olive oil, red wine vinegar, Dijon mustard, salt, and pepper.
3. Pour the dressing over the lentil mixture and toss to combine.

Arugula Salad with Pears and Goat Cheese

Ingredients:

- 4 cups arugula
- 1 ripe pear, sliced
- 1/4 cup goat cheese, crumbled
- 1/4 cup walnuts, toasted
- 2 tbsp balsamic vinaigrette

Instructions:

1. In a large bowl, combine arugula, pear slices, goat cheese, and walnuts.
2. Drizzle with balsamic vinaigrette and toss gently to combine.

Thai Cucumber Salad

Ingredients:

- 2 cups cucumber, thinly sliced
- 1/4 cup red onion, thinly sliced
- 1/4 cup chopped fresh cilantro
- 1/4 cup rice vinegar
- 1 tbsp sugar
- 1 tsp sesame oil
- Salt and pepper to taste

Instructions:

1. In a large bowl, combine cucumber, red onion, and cilantro.
2. In a small bowl, whisk together rice vinegar, sugar, sesame oil, salt, and pepper.
3. Pour the dressing over the cucumber mixture and toss to combine.

Bulgur Wheat Salad with Cherry Tomatoes

Ingredients:

- 1 cup bulgur wheat
- 1 1/2 cups boiling water
- 1 cup cherry tomatoes, halved
- 1/2 cup cucumber, diced
- 1/4 cup parsley, chopped
- 2 tbsp olive oil
- 1 tbsp lemon juice
- Salt and pepper to taste

Instructions:

1. In a bowl, combine bulgur wheat and boiling water. Cover and let sit for 15 minutes, then fluff with a fork.
2. In a large bowl, combine bulgur, cherry tomatoes, cucumber, and parsley.
3. In a small bowl, whisk together olive oil, lemon juice, salt, and pepper. Pour over the salad and toss gently to combine.

Broccoli and Raisin Salad

Ingredients:

- 4 cups broccoli florets
- 1/2 cup raisins
- 1/4 cup red onion, finely chopped
- 1/2 cup sunflower seeds
- 1/4 cup mayonnaise
- 1 tbsp apple cider vinegar
- Salt and pepper to taste

Instructions:

1. In a large bowl, combine broccoli florets, raisins, red onion, and sunflower seeds.
2. In a separate bowl, whisk together mayonnaise, apple cider vinegar, salt, and pepper.
3. Pour the dressing over the broccoli mixture and toss to combine.

Roasted Beet and Feta Salad

Ingredients:

- 2 cups roasted beets, diced
- 4 cups mixed greens
- 1/4 cup feta cheese, crumbled
- 1/4 cup walnuts, toasted
- 2 tbsp balsamic vinaigrette

Instructions:

1. In a large bowl, combine roasted beets, mixed greens, feta cheese, and walnuts.
2. Drizzle with balsamic vinaigrette and toss gently to combine.

Zucchini Noodle Salad with Pesto

Ingredients:

- 4 medium zucchinis, spiralized
- 1 cup cherry tomatoes, halved
- 1/2 cup basil pesto
- 1/4 cup pine nuts, toasted
- Salt and pepper to taste

Instructions:

1. In a large bowl, combine spiralized zucchini and cherry tomatoes.
2. Add pesto and toss until well coated.
3. Sprinkle with toasted pine nuts, and season with salt and pepper before serving.

Kale Salad with Lemon and Olive Oil

Ingredients:

- 4 cups kale, stems removed and chopped
- 1/4 cup olive oil
- 2 tbsp lemon juice
- Salt and pepper to taste
- 1/4 cup grated Parmesan cheese (optional)

Instructions:

1. In a large bowl, massage kale with olive oil, lemon juice, salt, and pepper until softened.
2. If desired, sprinkle with grated Parmesan cheese before serving.

Cucumber and Avocado Salad

Ingredients:

- 2 cucumbers, diced
- 1 avocado, diced
- 1/4 red onion, finely chopped
- 2 tbsp lime juice
- Salt and pepper to taste

Instructions:

1. In a bowl, combine cucumbers, avocado, and red onion.
2. Drizzle with lime juice, and season with salt and pepper. Toss gently to combine.

Pasta Salad with Spinach and Sun-Dried Tomatoes

Ingredients:

- 8 oz pasta (your choice)
- 2 cups fresh spinach
- 1/2 cup sun-dried tomatoes, chopped
- 1/4 cup feta cheese, crumbled
- 1/4 cup olive oil
- 2 tbsp balsamic vinegar
- Salt and pepper to taste

Instructions:

1. Cook pasta according to package instructions; drain and cool.
2. In a large bowl, combine cooked pasta, spinach, sun-dried tomatoes, and feta cheese.
3. In a small bowl, whisk together olive oil, balsamic vinegar, salt, and pepper, then pour over the salad and toss to combine.

Chopped Salad with Italian Dressing

Ingredients:

- 2 cups romaine lettuce, chopped
- 1 cup cherry tomatoes, halved
- 1/2 cucumber, diced
- 1/2 red onion, chopped
- 1/4 cup Italian dressing
- Salt and pepper to taste

Instructions:

1. In a large bowl, combine romaine lettuce, cherry tomatoes, cucumber, and red onion.
2. Drizzle with Italian dressing, and season with salt and pepper. Toss well to combine.

Citrus Salad with Grapefruit and Orange

Ingredients:

- 2 grapefruits, segmented
- 2 oranges, segmented
- 1/4 red onion, thinly sliced
- 1/4 cup mint leaves, chopped
- 1 tbsp honey (optional)

Instructions:

1. In a large bowl, combine grapefruit segments, orange segments, red onion, and mint leaves.
2. If desired, drizzle with honey and toss gently to combine.

Asian Noodle Salad

Ingredients:

- 8 oz soba noodles (or rice noodles)
- 1 cup shredded carrots
- 1 bell pepper, thinly sliced
- 1 cup snap peas
- 1/4 cup soy sauce
- 2 tbsp sesame oil
- 1 tbsp rice vinegar
- 1 tbsp sesame seeds

Instructions:

1. Cook noodles according to package instructions; drain and cool.
2. In a large bowl, combine cooled noodles, carrots, bell pepper, and snap peas.
3. In a small bowl, whisk together soy sauce, sesame oil, rice vinegar, and sesame seeds, then pour over the salad and toss to combine.

Berry Spinach Salad with Almonds

Ingredients:

- 4 cups fresh spinach
- 1 cup mixed berries (strawberries, blueberries, raspberries)
- 1/4 cup sliced almonds, toasted
- 1/4 cup feta cheese, crumbled
- 2 tbsp balsamic vinaigrette

Instructions:

1. In a large bowl, combine spinach, mixed berries, sliced almonds, and feta cheese.
2. Drizzle with balsamic vinaigrette and toss gently to combine.

Sweet Potato and Black Bean Salad

Ingredients:

- 2 medium sweet potatoes, peeled and cubed
- 1 can (15 oz) black beans, rinsed and drained
- 1 red bell pepper, diced
- 1/4 cup red onion, finely chopped
- 1/4 cup cilantro, chopped
- 3 tbsp olive oil
- 2 tbsp lime juice
- Salt and pepper to taste

Instructions:

1. Preheat the oven to 400°F (200°C). Toss sweet potato cubes with olive oil, salt, and pepper, then spread on a baking sheet and roast for 20-25 minutes until tender.
2. In a large bowl, combine roasted sweet potatoes, black beans, red bell pepper, red onion, and cilantro.
3. Drizzle with lime juice, toss gently to combine, and serve warm or at room temperature.

Cabbage and Apple Salad

Ingredients:

- 4 cups green cabbage, thinly sliced
- 1 apple, cored and thinly sliced
- 1/4 cup raisins
- 1/4 cup walnuts, chopped
- 1/4 cup apple cider vinegar
- 2 tbsp honey
- Salt and pepper to taste

Instructions:

1. In a large bowl, combine sliced cabbage, apple, raisins, and walnuts.
2. In a small bowl, whisk together apple cider vinegar, honey, salt, and pepper.
3. Pour dressing over the salad, toss well to combine, and let sit for 15 minutes before serving.

Roasted Chickpea Salad

Ingredients:

- 1 can (15 oz) chickpeas, rinsed and drained
- 1 tsp paprika
- 1 tsp cumin
- 2 cups mixed greens
- 1/2 cucumber, diced
- 1/4 cup red onion, finely chopped
- 3 tbsp tahini
- 2 tbsp lemon juice
- Salt and pepper to taste

Instructions:

1. Preheat the oven to 400°F (200°C). Toss chickpeas with olive oil, paprika, cumin, salt, and pepper, then spread on a baking sheet and roast for 20-25 minutes until crispy.
2. In a large bowl, combine mixed greens, cucumber, red onion, and roasted chickpeas.
3. In a small bowl, whisk together tahini, lemon juice, and water to thin, then drizzle over the salad and toss to combine.

Corn and Tomato Salad

Ingredients:

- 2 cups fresh corn kernels (or 1 can, drained)
- 1 cup cherry tomatoes, halved
- 1/4 cup red onion, finely chopped
- 1/4 cup cilantro, chopped
- 3 tbsp olive oil
- 2 tbsp lime juice
- Salt and pepper to taste

Instructions:

1. In a large bowl, combine corn, cherry tomatoes, red onion, and cilantro.
2. Drizzle with olive oil and lime juice, season with salt and pepper, and toss gently to combine.

Hummus and Veggie Salad

Ingredients:

- 1 cup hummus (store-bought or homemade)
- 1 cucumber, diced
- 1 bell pepper, diced
- 1 carrot, shredded
- 1 cup cherry tomatoes, halved
- 1/4 cup parsley, chopped

Instructions:

1. In a large bowl, combine diced cucumber, bell pepper, shredded carrot, cherry tomatoes, and parsley.
2. Serve vegetables with hummus as a dip or mix hummus into the salad for a creamy texture.

Pea Salad with Bacon and Cheese

Ingredients:

- 3 cups frozen peas, thawed
- 1/2 cup cooked bacon, crumbled
- 1/2 cup cheddar cheese, shredded
- 1/4 cup red onion, finely chopped
- 1/4 cup mayonnaise
- 1 tbsp apple cider vinegar
- Salt and pepper to taste

Instructions:

1. In a large bowl, combine thawed peas, crumbled bacon, cheddar cheese, and red onion.
2. In a small bowl, whisk together mayonnaise, apple cider vinegar, salt, and pepper, then pour over the salad and toss to combine.

Carrot and Raisin Salad

Ingredients:

- 3 cups carrots, grated
- 1/2 cup raisins
- 1/4 cup walnuts, chopped
- 1/4 cup mayonnaise
- 2 tbsp honey
- Salt to taste

Instructions:

1. In a large bowl, combine grated carrots, raisins, and walnuts.
2. In a small bowl, whisk together mayonnaise, honey, and salt, then pour over the salad and toss to combine.

Fruit Salad with Mint

Ingredients:

- 2 cups mixed berries (strawberries, blueberries, raspberries)
- 1 cup grapes, halved
- 2 kiwis, peeled and diced
- 1 orange, segmented
- 1/4 cup fresh mint leaves, chopped
- 1 tbsp honey (optional)

Instructions:

1. In a large bowl, combine mixed berries, grapes, kiwis, and orange segments.
2. If desired, drizzle with honey and sprinkle with chopped mint before serving.

Fattoush Salad

Ingredients:

- 2 cups mixed greens
- 1 cucumber, diced
- 2 tomatoes, diced
- 1 radish, sliced
- 1 bell pepper, diced
- 1/4 cup red onion, chopped
- 1/4 cup parsley, chopped
- 1/4 cup mint leaves, chopped
- 2 pita breads, toasted and broken into pieces
- 3 tbsp olive oil
- 2 tbsp lemon juice
- Salt and pepper to taste

Instructions:

1. In a large bowl, combine mixed greens, cucumber, tomatoes, radish, bell pepper, red onion, parsley, and mint.
2. Add the toasted pita pieces.
3. In a small bowl, whisk together olive oil, lemon juice, salt, and pepper, then drizzle over the salad and toss to combine.

Radish and Cucumber Salad

Ingredients:

- 1 cucumber, sliced
- 1 cup radishes, thinly sliced
- 1/4 cup red onion, thinly sliced
- 2 tbsp dill, chopped
- 3 tbsp olive oil
- 2 tbsp vinegar (white or apple cider)
- Salt and pepper to taste

Instructions:

1. In a bowl, combine cucumber, radishes, red onion, and dill.
2. In a separate bowl, whisk together olive oil, vinegar, salt, and pepper.
3. Pour the dressing over the salad and toss gently to combine.

Smashed Chickpea Salad

Ingredients:

- 1 can (15 oz) chickpeas, rinsed and drained
- 1/4 cup red onion, finely chopped
- 1/4 cup cucumber, diced
- 1/4 cup parsley, chopped
- 2 tbsp lemon juice
- 2 tbsp tahini
- Salt and pepper to taste

Instructions:

1. In a bowl, lightly mash the chickpeas with a fork, leaving some whole.
2. Add red onion, cucumber, parsley, lemon juice, tahini, salt, and pepper, and mix to combine.

Mediterranean Orzo Salad

Ingredients:

- 1 cup orzo pasta, cooked and cooled
- 1 cup cherry tomatoes, halved
- 1/2 cucumber, diced
- 1/4 cup red onion, chopped
- 1/2 cup feta cheese, crumbled
- 1/4 cup olives, pitted and sliced
- 3 tbsp olive oil
- 2 tbsp lemon juice
- Salt and pepper to taste

Instructions:

1. In a large bowl, combine cooked orzo, cherry tomatoes, cucumber, red onion, feta cheese, and olives.
2. Drizzle with olive oil and lemon juice, and season with salt and pepper, then toss to combine.

Tomato and Mozzarella Salad

Ingredients:

- 2 large tomatoes, sliced
- 8 oz fresh mozzarella, sliced
- 1/4 cup fresh basil leaves
- 3 tbsp olive oil
- 2 tbsp balsamic vinegar
- Salt and pepper to taste

Instructions:

1. On a platter, alternate layers of tomato and mozzarella slices.
2. Scatter basil leaves over the top.
3. Drizzle with olive oil and balsamic vinegar, and season with salt and pepper before serving.

Spicy Kale Salad with Tahini Dressing

Ingredients:

- 4 cups kale, stems removed and chopped
- 1/2 cup carrot, shredded
- 1/4 cup red cabbage, shredded
- 1/4 cup almonds, sliced
- 3 tbsp tahini
- 2 tbsp lemon juice
- 1 tsp sriracha (or to taste)
- Salt and pepper to taste

Instructions:

1. In a large bowl, combine kale, carrot, red cabbage, and almonds.
2. In a small bowl, whisk together tahini, lemon juice, sriracha, salt, and pepper, adding water as needed to thin.
3. Pour dressing over the salad, toss well, and serve.

Egg Salad with Spinach

Ingredients:

- 4 hard-boiled eggs, chopped
- 2 cups fresh spinach, chopped
- 1/4 cup mayonnaise
- 1 tbsp mustard
- Salt and pepper to taste
- 1/4 cup green onions, chopped (optional)

Instructions:

1. In a bowl, combine chopped eggs and spinach.
2. Add mayonnaise, mustard, salt, and pepper, mixing gently to combine.
3. Stir in green onions if using, and serve on bread or as a side.

Sesame Ginger Salad

Ingredients:

- 2 cups mixed greens
- 1 cup shredded cabbage
- 1 carrot, shredded
- 1/4 cup red bell pepper, sliced
- 2 tbsp sesame seeds
- 3 tbsp sesame oil
- 2 tbsp rice vinegar
- 1 tbsp soy sauce
- Salt and pepper to taste

Instructions:

1. In a large bowl, combine mixed greens, cabbage, carrot, bell pepper, and sesame seeds.
2. In a small bowl, whisk together sesame oil, rice vinegar, soy sauce, salt, and pepper.
3. Drizzle dressing over the salad, toss to combine, and serve.

Roasted Vegetable Salad

Ingredients:

- 2 cups mixed vegetables (zucchini, bell peppers, carrots, etc.), chopped
- 2 tbsp olive oil
- Salt and pepper to taste
- 4 cups mixed greens
- 1/4 cup feta cheese, crumbled
- 1/4 cup balsamic vinaigrette

Instructions:

1. Preheat the oven to 425°F (220°C).
2. Toss chopped vegetables with olive oil, salt, and pepper. Spread on a baking sheet and roast for 20-25 minutes until tender.
3. In a large bowl, combine mixed greens and roasted vegetables.
4. Top with feta cheese and drizzle with balsamic vinaigrette before serving.

Nicoise Salad

Ingredients:

- 2 cups mixed greens
- 1/2 cup green beans, blanched
- 1/2 cup cherry tomatoes, halved
- 1/4 cup red onion, sliced
- 1 can (5 oz) tuna, drained
- 2 hard-boiled eggs, quartered
- 1/4 cup olives
- 3 tbsp olive oil
- 2 tbsp red wine vinegar
- Salt and pepper to taste

Instructions:

1. In a large bowl, layer mixed greens, green beans, cherry tomatoes, red onion, tuna, eggs, and olives.
2. In a small bowl, whisk together olive oil, red wine vinegar, salt, and pepper.
3. Drizzle the dressing over the salad and serve.

Taco Salad with Ground Turkey

Ingredients:

- 1 lb ground turkey
- 1 tbsp taco seasoning
- 4 cups romaine lettuce, chopped
- 1 cup cherry tomatoes, halved
- 1 cup corn (canned or frozen)
- 1/2 cup black beans, rinsed and drained
- 1/4 cup shredded cheese
- 1/4 cup salsa
- 1 avocado, diced

Instructions:

1. In a skillet, cook ground turkey until browned, then stir in taco seasoning and cook according to package instructions.
2. In a large bowl, combine lettuce, cherry tomatoes, corn, black beans, and cooked turkey.
3. Top with shredded cheese, salsa, and diced avocado before serving.

Rice Salad with Peas and Carrots

Ingredients:

- 2 cups cooked rice (white or brown)
- 1 cup peas (fresh or frozen)
- 1 cup carrots, diced
- 1/4 cup red onion, diced
- 3 tbsp olive oil
- 2 tbsp lemon juice
- Salt and pepper to taste

Instructions:

1. In a large bowl, combine cooked rice, peas, carrots, and red onion.
2. In a small bowl, whisk together olive oil, lemon juice, salt, and pepper.
3. Drizzle the dressing over the rice mixture and toss to combine.

Quinoa Tabbouleh

Ingredients:

- 1 cup cooked quinoa, cooled
- 1 cup parsley, chopped
- 1/2 cup mint leaves, chopped
- 1 cucumber, diced
- 2 tomatoes, diced
- 3 tbsp olive oil
- 2 tbsp lemon juice
- Salt and pepper to taste

Instructions:

1. In a large bowl, combine cooked quinoa, parsley, mint, cucumber, and tomatoes.
2. In a small bowl, whisk together olive oil, lemon juice, salt, and pepper.
3. Pour the dressing over the quinoa salad and mix well.

Lime Chicken Salad

Ingredients:

- 2 cups cooked chicken, shredded
- 4 cups mixed greens
- 1/2 cup black beans, rinsed and drained
- 1/2 cup corn (canned or frozen)
- 1/4 cup red onion, sliced
- 1 avocado, diced
- 3 tbsp lime juice
- 2 tbsp olive oil
- Salt and pepper to taste

Instructions:

1. In a large bowl, combine shredded chicken, mixed greens, black beans, corn, red onion, and avocado.
2. In a small bowl, whisk together lime juice, olive oil, salt, and pepper.
3. Drizzle the dressing over the salad and toss gently to combine.

Chopped Greek Salad

Ingredients:

- 2 cups romaine lettuce, chopped
- 1 cucumber, diced
- 1 cup cherry tomatoes, halved
- 1/4 cup red onion, diced
- 1/2 cup feta cheese, crumbled
- 1/4 cup kalamata olives, pitted and sliced
- 3 tbsp olive oil
- 2 tbsp red wine vinegar
- Salt and pepper to taste

Instructions:

1. In a large bowl, combine romaine lettuce, cucumber, cherry tomatoes, red onion, feta cheese, and olives.
2. In a small bowl, whisk together olive oil, red wine vinegar, salt, and pepper.
3. Drizzle the dressing over the salad and toss to combine.

Pineapple and Avocado Salad

Ingredients:

- 2 cups mixed greens
- 1 cup pineapple, diced
- 1 avocado, diced
- 1/4 cup red onion, thinly sliced
- 2 tbsp lime juice
- 3 tbsp olive oil
- Salt and pepper to taste

Instructions:

1. In a large bowl, combine mixed greens, pineapple, avocado, and red onion.
2. In a small bowl, whisk together lime juice, olive oil, salt, and pepper.
3. Drizzle the dressing over the salad and toss gently before serving.

Zesty Lime Shrimp Salad

Ingredients:

- 1 lb shrimp, peeled and deveined
- 2 tbsp olive oil
- 1 lime, juiced
- 2 cups mixed greens
- 1/2 cup cherry tomatoes, halved
- 1/4 cup red onion, thinly sliced
- 1 avocado, diced
- Salt and pepper to taste

Instructions:

1. In a skillet, heat olive oil over medium heat. Add shrimp and cook until pink and opaque, about 3-4 minutes.
2. Remove from heat and toss with lime juice, salt, and pepper.
3. In a large bowl, combine mixed greens, cherry tomatoes, red onion, and avocado.
4. Add cooked shrimp on top and serve.

Mango and Black Bean Salad

Ingredients:

- 1 ripe mango, diced
- 1 can (15 oz) black beans, rinsed and drained
- 1/2 red bell pepper, diced
- 1/4 cup red onion, diced
- 1/4 cup cilantro, chopped
- 2 tbsp lime juice
- 1 tbsp olive oil
- Salt and pepper to taste

Instructions:

1. In a large bowl, combine mango, black beans, red bell pepper, red onion, and cilantro.
2. In a small bowl, whisk together lime juice, olive oil, salt, and pepper.
3. Pour the dressing over the salad and toss gently to combine before serving.